I0756256

FINISHING LINE PRESS
www.finishinglinepress.com

Lately

poems by

Charles S. Cobean

Finishing Line Press
Georgetown, Kentucky

Lately

Knowledge is visible … it might be seen in the daily world.
—Mark Doty

The end of man is knowledge, but there is one thing he can't know.
He can't know whether knowledge will save him or kill him.
—Robert Penn Warren

ISBN 979-8-89990-392-2 First Edition

ACKNOWLEDGMENTS

I would like to thank the following journals and their editors for agreeing to publish poems that appear in this collection:

Rattle: Cul-de-sacs
Poets Online: Accounting, Stupid Hats
The Brownstone Poets Anthology: I Have This Life
MORIA: Lately, Santa Amnesia (nominated for a 2025 Pushcart Prize)
Fixed and Free Quarterly: Scar Tissue, If She Will, Five Pages, Climbing Out, Blood-Bright Futures (Scenes from a Reunion), Revenants, I Have Issues with God

I would especially like to thank the many poets whose workshops I have attended, and to the leaders of the open mic campfires I have read at, whose generosity of spirit contributed to the work here, one word at a time: Kim Addonizio, Amie Whittemore, Dorianne Laux, Ada Limón, Lauren Camp, Ellen Bass, Major Jackson, Gary McDowell, Alicia Ostriker, Billy Brown, and Patricia Carragon, among others.

I also want to thank my friend and weekly sounding board, Josephine LoRe, whose insights and feedback continue to be invaluable.

Publisher: Leah Huete de Maines
Editor: Christen Kincaid
Cover Art: Charles S. Cobean
Author Photo: Robert Cobean
Cover Design: Elizabeth Maines McCleavy

Order online: www.finishinglinepress.com
also available on amazon.com

Author inquiries and mail orders:
Finishing Line Press
PO Box 1626
Georgetown, Kentucky 40324
USA

Contents

Scar Tissue

We come to each other like this
with unclaimed freight scars and marks blazes

our diaries open tattooed on ankles and arms
beneath chins beside eyes on both knees

everyone has fallen
this I think is what love is

Listening

He could not hear the dusk fall
over the river just a high bee-hum

that wasn't it nor hear the stoplight
by the drugstore whining in the instant

before it changed to *go* like a prophecy
that never missed
                                        one evening the president

was dead and we stood together out back
near the creek the two of us and saw

but only I heard the barred owl in last light
glide between the oaks and hickories

and we witnessed the fireflies bob and weave
like buoys in the channels above the grass

but this too he could not hear as if
there were no space left at all for listening

this did not seem fair though what did then
yet when the time came many years later

and night opened up in front of him like a shaft
and roared he turned his ear toward it

If She Will

A child leaves a handful and comes back a fist.
Who but his mother, who has watched the door
Greek-like for his return, and never given up
her each-day's wondering, her longing;
who but she can take his knuckled heart
and the knowledge it holds of sadness
and bury it out back like the hills bury the moon?

Who but she can burrow the clammy black soil
then fold it over and pat it down and wait for spring
and the cave-pale shoots, all five, for they will be fist no more
and stand there with him in the gelling light
and remark on each yearning tendril?

Who but she, who loves him, who has sworn to love him
who has bathed him in love, anointed him with its sacred oil
poured it over his hair and combed it carefully through
though he complained and would not sit still;
who has fed him bowls full, hot, with a pinch of pepper and sage;
listened to his prayers, felt his forehead;
pulled the quilt over his shoulders in the cold night.
Who but she can do such things for him, again, if she will?

Let us say the world hangs on it, or a piece of the world
their world, their shared world, their patient shared world.

And when next he proceeds, alone, without maps
as she knows he will, for that is his nature, which she loves;
when again he follows stars and rivers and roads;
when he crosses the oceans and borders of countries
so old they have forgotten how to dream;
when he walks where no one loves him
he will still be able to love himself
and she can let him go.

After His Death

Cages opened in her grief. Through thickets, feral things ravening and stalking.

As flame fills spirit. As spirit consumes self.

Hers was not the grief of a woman with years. Having been kissed by
presidents, christened ships, sipped the monks' Himalayan tea.

Prayer could not hope to contain it. Nor whispers of priests and friends.
Children.

So, he stayed, hung around, didn't go. Sank her grief deep within himself
and drifted there in the room that still echoed with his name.

One night, he sang to her with singed-wing voice the old *vaquero* songs.
A kiss in her sleep.

When the iron vanished, it was he who hid it behind his old sweaters
in the armoire and locked it.

His, the wet footprints on the tile. The red kettle at night whistling.

When she told us, we hardly knew what to think.

But sometimes even in our disbelief we would catch his scent. Mulled
spice and hydraulics.

When her years ended, she called to him. I saw him, I thought
over my shoulder.

My brother only, stepping closer, thinking she must have meant him.

Nonetheless I spoke. *He is waiting*, I said, and hoped I wasn't wrong.

And another voice that wasn't mine said, *Jeanie*. And she lowered
her lids half-mast and went.

@youmail.com

I'm writing you this instead of a letter
because you are without hands now

and who would tear open the envelope
nor have you eyes to read

so I will use my inside voice
and speak in pictures

it's a good time of day morning my favorite
the light through the window

the color of *Weißwein* the sweet kind
that comes with a headache

and it's early enough that my thoughts
haven't drowned yet in the riptide

that rushes in and pulls me out
past the sandbars

I have learned not to fight it anymore
swim sideways until it lets me go

I wanted to tell you that your children
no longer speak and that I dreamed

you were still here holding us together
and my brother still my brother

I should also mention
I have a grandson now and one of his names

is yours which means in the tradition
his parents wish upon him your better traits

though they are taking my word
on just what those are

don't be sad I remember for them
but he has many names this boy

so I hope yours doesn't get lost
in the long bright string of them

you might like to hear that time
has finally stopped for me or else

slowed down enough to notice it or maybe
just elongated like the summer light

my throat thirsts for like this morning's light
the light I mentioned

I know you didn't see the morning
the night when all your words were left

without breath to hold them up
and there was a buzzing emptiness

where the room had been and you realized
you didn't understand anything

the way you thought you had
I wondered if you wondered

if what you did and didn't do
was worth the wake you left spreading

in our tiny quarry lake
though this would have been a pointless question

what else have we known except everything
we've ever had what else are you

except the boat we keep sailing
and anyway it would have never occurred to you

to ask such a doleful thing to even wonder
and instead let the vacancy take you

like an outgoing wave not fight it
so I guess the voice you hear is just me

answering my own questions
yes it's unsettling to write like this

one-sided into the still dry air of my room
and maybe not my best idea

I wouldn't want to put words in your mouth
though now that I think about it

I do

Birds

I think of her when birds pip outside an open window
small birds with high lilting voices like hers
and charming warbles no harsh caws or squawks

I think how her voice changed after her fall and the bleed
deep and coarse not at all bird-like
as if she were already speaking from a fearful place

she called in her rough new voice to my father who no longer was
or was it to her oldest son with the same name
my brother

then she stopped speaking and it no longer mattered
still her lips moved as if singing to herself
remembering all the words where they went

it wasn't true not entirely I came out of expectations
hovering bedside with my brother and my sister
for the end that hung like a cold moon over our shoulders

but I think it was true entirely true of my brother
who lived in singed silence
and brooded over his place in things his impermanence

I don't think he understood she forgave him
as his mother for his fury and discontent
each day

and that each day he needed it a little more
and that now it was his turn to forgive called to the rail
for a child must forgive his mother

whose pity and fear for her first-born surely cut but did not slay him
whose unkindness to our father at the last
was only the air around her growing wet with ash

out in the hall a nurse whispered *another two weeks*
so my brother went home and missed his chance
he nearly missed the inurnment too

appearing late in a Lyft in haphazard clothes
I think of him my brother now even now years later
how that sepsis still wrings his gut out like a towel

how he finds birdsong so disquieting

I Count to Four

—for Josephine LoRe

I.

This morning, pouring my ration
I counted to four—a tidy measurement, a mug half-full
and that's all it took, *easy as that*

to summon forth the day's optimism
though it doesn't last, never does
which is to say caffeine wears off like everything else.

Which means, I have to remind myself
there's always tomorrow.
Because four is a virtuous little number.

For instance, last night, *what luck,* I counted four naked
-eye planets, and late February, on the deck
I counted four red finches

and knew for certain it was a prayer of spring.
And yet whose prayers are truly answered?
Do you see my problem here?

Days go by, even in spring, which is vociferous in these parts
where I do not leave the house
where my half-cup tilts toward emptiness

and I begin to realize how far it is to the end
of the driveway where the mailbox leans slightly to the left
and how, when I try to speak, yesterday's words

reshuffle like furniture for an open house.
By this I mean I repeat myself.
But what are words

when everyone has stopped listening—
winter flies rousing in the glass
useless in their way.

II.

Drop by drop, hope's canteen runs dry
and entire days march by in black columns

and who can tell one from another.
Counting fails to lift me—

four are the fingers of an un-whole hand
four is the family that used to be five

four is grief without acceptance.
Because four is a vulturous little number.

Listen, the dead tried their best, I do not fault them
all their pockets turned out, emptied of blame.

And isn't forgetting another name for forgiveness?
Still, I would rather have them here and not there

outside time, vaporous, hiking the dark road.
I would rather have my mother and father

around instead of their things: her nightstand
and his watch upon it with its heartbeats

its crepitations, its footsteps—
toward *what*, backwards to *what else?*

III.
I did not think this would be about grief when I started out
though it always seems to come to that, for who of us
does not hear rumors of pain? By that I mean, optimism
fades and does not rise each time I hold my breath
while the CRT sings its valorous little numbers to my parts.
You look surprised. Did I not tell you? My apologies.
Truthfully, I would rather be folding laundry, keeping
the towels and t-shirts neat in drawers I can understand
unlike my fears, which are ants pouring in and out
of the holes in the world and can never be counted.

IV.
I think about space-time, its continuum
and wonder if the dead are constrained
by its various properties. Must they mill
about the places where we left them?

Or can they vault like star-men beyond
the speed of consciousness? Do they see
the past and present dancing together
like lovers in a ballroom of untold dimension?

And if not, if they are stuck in some more
finite space, even if only our memory
are they happiest when we drop by?
Are they waiting there for us now

in the fulsome count of days?

Between Us

Our dead come between us drift in
like cold air under the doors and gather

fathers mothers a sister a child unnamed
friends from school from work

in the Towers in the river in the air
all dead all between us

the words between us calculate like digits
in long columns adding up

denials slights small betrayals outright lies
indifferently tossed with aim and intent

piling up like cordwood like fence posts
like the ridge rising in the bed

like the drifts of leaves
blown against the hedges

all dead all between us
how do we go on?

Five Pages

Last night I tried starting something
since it's been a while years I think
and she was wearing that white t-shirt
with all the holes in it which I took
as a signal and yet it turned out
that rolling her way and sliding
my ever-hopeful hand up her arm
toward her shoulder was not at all
the message she was beaming out
we're missing five pages of love
she said in that voice as if love was
a book I didn't know she'd read and
wished now she hadn't given away
and I wondered what could possibly
be on those pages and why had I
never seen them and if after all that
perhaps they'd been meant
in the first place for someone else
my friends happiness it seems is
everywhere and reasonably priced
like pyrite at a local rock shop
but love—love the irresistible sun
that bends you to it like a stalk
that's another story

Cul-de-sacs

My love it is time to admit I was right
about cul-de-sacs and how the absence
of through-traffic and speed bumps
and yellow caution signs is preferable
to the occasionally inattentive
and the curious or the dumb-lost
who wander down our small arched street
even if they use our driveway
to turn around and wander back
I can't tell you how gratifying it is
to be right about something
when I was just as likely to be wrong
there's much guesswork in the decision
-making process you know fifty-fifty at best
my love this was before you knew me
but back in my drinking days
I used to hand out fortunes in bars
like a boozy Johnny Appleseed because
it had dawned on me those fortunes
I'd so carefully collected might not be
mine to keep after all and I should find
their rightful owners and give them back
the wing-shaped seeds of their future
for who would want to be accused
of having waited too long for
success to finally come their way
or to *settle at last into happiness*
after a lifetime of change
and who of us doesn't need hope
but in case you're wondering
I kept the one I knew was meant for me
the one that said *this person's love*
is just and true and you may rely on it
it was you my love that cheap piece
of paper was prophesizing
and wasn't I right about that
for a while

Accounting

So that each story in its telling may summon its fate—
was this the instant when what lay ahead was hard-set—
and we may thus come to better understand ourselves, our journey
we must begin to ask questions.

Now that you are alone, what are your days like?
Each day I rise and drink from the chilled flask of a thousand desires.
Each night I toss within the plaid cotton grumble of a thousand
    second-guesses.
In these days and nights, I find that solitude is the one unflawed mirror
even when I do not recognize the face.

Looking back, how would you assess your life?
Luck. But there is no accounting for luck, is there?
Or luck piled on luck, or the reverse: luck all run out.

Do you miss work?
I miss my fellow workers.

Do you miss your fellow workers?
No. I never see them.

Who do you miss?
I miss my father.
There was never enough of him, and now there is none.
His unfilled/unfillable gloves rolled in the pockets of my winter coat
with my keys and an old mint.
I miss asking his advice—my *if this, if that.*

Who do you miss?
I miss my mother.
She surrounds me, even now, a blue-eyed ocean.
But I cannot say she was a good mother.
Words from her only ever meant loss, or was it less?
Still, when I was sick, she brought me canned soup and honey toast.
I miss loving her.

Did you reach the country of your dreams?
I reached the end of the map, if that is what you mean.
It was drier than I imagined: arroyos, mounds and rocks
    speechless petroglyphs

like a cigarette had burned a hole in it.
And no one was there but an older self; sadness wrapped him up like a fish.
Now there are new selves I am fonder of, each with his own map.

What then of the future?
The future will not confess itself.
Yet I sleep certain knowing night will thin and the sky will be new again.
Isn't that enough?

And what of love?
Ah, love! Love no longer fills me, though how can I not yearn for it again?

Reckonings (First Kiss)

My first kiss has died, cirrhosis of the liver.
Her ex-best friend emailed the news
aggrieved still, not grieving: my feelings

too. But I think instead of there, I should
begin here, with her smile: crooked
before braces, how it glinted

under the streetlight where we had stopped
our bikes in the drawn-out summer dusk
and how we leaned them both together

to make an "A," a roof for our handlebars
still in hand, and closed our eyes. I should add
that we missed and tried again and once

or twice got it right. The darkening street
seemed to flash and spin, and, *oh*, how could
either of us breathe? She was a head taller

widely admired, with real boobs, and older
by a year or two, but not so much she should
be embarrassed. I was special, plucked

from an orchard of apple-faced boys
and we spent all summer together, poolside
at the Club. Now the years between us are

nothing but a single step across a shallow stream
that I could ford at any time, join her there
if I wish, or accident befall, or lightning strike.

Or like her, drink myself to death.

Blood-Bright Futures (Scenes from a Reunion)

Near the top step
below the plaza strung with bulbs
our most recent classmate to pass
across her sorrow still fresh
stands watch for late arrivals like me

how relieved I am to see her
since we hadn't said goodbye
and I rise toward her
like a salmon flung upriver

she twists her neck a bit my way
and grins and says my name
her voice bathes me
in the old water
perfectly warm

I want to stay and ask her
what she does most days
now that time is endless
and she is not driven so much
by usefulness

but I am already too late
for she has bent her eyes back
to the horizon and the others still breathing
on the long flight up
so I climb past her
wordless again

I hope that seeing her there will be enough
and some behind me will see her too
and hear their names spoken
for that is the joy of this
why we still attend
when all we see
is death

friends I know
I know how lucky we are to have made it this far
here where no one wants our unhappiness
where none of us are considered fallen
or out of season
out of context

where we carry the mirror that loves us best
and a basin in which to rinse our pain
where we laugh carelessly at ourselves
and our scorned sclerotic hearts

and though there are expiration dates everywhere
and the food is not-warm but everybody eats
and the music good but nobody dances
for the time we are together
our blood-bright futures
remain outside
lingering
on the
steps

Unfinished Business

My dead show up with fists
of unclaimed freight unfinished business
pressed tight to their chests
their dreams slice across mine like snowplows
dreams so sleek and transparent
they can't hide what they want

my late first kiss wants to kiss me again
beneath the streetlight out front of her parents' house
and my backyard friend who drowned in the river
the river that should have held him to the shore
that held him instead entangled in the channel
below his father's boat
he wants to sail together like before
before I made excuses and lived

or the aunt who loved me without a single condition
wants to assure me she's seen worse
worse than *this* and my uncle the captain
who handed down orders unheeded
by his sons his five mutinous sons
and three of them buried before him
just wants me to listen

and my father who lost at sea all the sea
-green fields of my childhood
my childhood that echoed without him
wants to teach me the proper way to shave
to miter trim break a horse locate Polaris
as if it were not too late

and my mother my beautiful self
-involved mother with her need for forgiveness
wants to make amends
her smile rearranges me like furniture
until I'm not sure where guests will sit
she gives me what is no longer hers to give
the late light that blazes all around us
the air so sharp it hurts just to breathe
and we drink in the old affection
like mulled wine

Revenants

When asked, each seems shrouded in some unhappiness
impatient with the places they exist
and the future
that never seems to come.

One misses the sun.
Another misses the sky that frames the sun.
Another has never known anything but infinite darkness.
Still another says she cannot find her god among all the others.

In one sad case, the bright window of promise and expectation
closed too soon, or so she says.
Another lies pinned under the immense snowdrift of history
although perhaps this is only his past.

One says that just before the alarm
he dreamt of waking, then woke
into emptiness
from which he has been unable to wake.

I am thinking now of inviting them all for coffee
by flashlight and candle, camp stove
as we did with our neighbors
when the great temblor shook the chimney onto the roof

and the refrigerator onto the linoleum
with the shattered cups and bottles
and all of us out
into the cul-de-sac we shared.

It shook us like a branch full of rain
and we met in the darkness
and the sudden silence of everything
that kept us from hearing one another until then.

Climbing Out

Some nights absence lays down alongside
and inhales your shadow leaves a hole

you cannot see and cannot fill
to fall into when the room tilts like vertigo

but it is not eyes that leap up to shimmy
on the dance floor of distance not hands

that cat-claw the empty air for rail limb gutter
denial excuse drape vine to hold onto

on the way down
                                        Katayama-san who knew
a thing or two about absence and balance

and climbing out and the tender red bridge
that spans *here* and *there* once counseled

on a vertiginous swaying road in the Hida
Mountains *best to close eyes raise chin*

breathe calming breath
ne?

Cheap Laminate

I think my dreams are trying to tell me something
that my own pleasure embarrasses me
and the three women I swear love me don't
and the echo I hear is my own hallooing emptiness

it seems there's been a hard turn of late
toward revelation
and I can't move my arms
to ward it off

toward dawn my oldest friend three years dead
appeared in fading blue distance
and drowned me in fathoms
of advice I mean what did I ever do
to him except not be him
not call out to him not intercede
watch instead his splintering tornadic path
from across the road
for who can cross fate
just ask the Greeks
and besides you can get life-advice
from anyone even idiots if you ask
and I didn't ask

but at least I could hear his voice

which means there must be some half
-decent take-away available like maybe
this is a *when the student is ready*
kind of moment and there's a chance the long
-layered night might crack like a walnut
and let me go

I'm saying time shreds
like cheap laminate and too soon
and no one knows himself
and what he might do
and since the world takes the trouble
to lay out a bed for me
I may as well
get in

Lately

Lately, I've been showing up at reunions
not my own and somehow know everyone.

By that I mean I know no one
and remember no one's name.

Meaning I suspect these new friends are just
my old friends in hastily assembled frames.

Meaning their new throats gargle with old words
and the familiar radiance of their voices opens in the air

in front of me like butterflies, as if time and distance
had not stretched between us like a hedge.

This makes me wonder if all-time is one-time, an ocean
and I am standing in it up to my waist.

And if I am awake in dreams, do I ever wake from them
or do they simply at some point close into darkness.

And who anyway is responsible but one's own impenetrable soul
and not God for the content of his dreams?

Lately, I've been thinking of aging in terms of exile.
Is this happening to you like it's happening to me?

Like when your children grow and are gone
and you finally run out of parents.

And the sound of footsteps is the sound of leaving
not coming, and grief swims close, just below the ice.

Which brings me to this: I am trying hard to remember
when love was still good and tasted like cinnamon.

I am trying to remember when skin was fragrant
and baby-soft, and I hated to leave it.

My love, I closed my eyes when we kissed
and missed the chance to memorize yours

close-up, and lately, when I think of you
your eyes are all the wrong color.

This is also what I mean by exile.
Or is this me thinking only of myself again?

Santa Amnesia

Last week, my father's birthday slid past
unnoticed. It was also his death
-day and the anniversary of my first marriage
so you'd think I'd remember. I confess
I have tried my best to forget
that godforsaken anniversary
but cannot, linked irreversibly as it is
to my father's parentheticals
which seem important to remember
like the names of the capitals, saints, winter birds.
They say this is how it starts, the wrestling
with the days of the week, proper nouns.
I would like to know just who *they* are
so we might have a word or two.
Preferably without nouns.
Time drifts, a boat without sails.
Memory mills about like the unemployed
waiting for a good day's labor.
Blessed Mother, is this the beginning of *l'oublie*?
Will I remember the faces of my children?
I can see my birds are leaving their branches.
Must I rely on dreams now to lead me
to warmer climes? Even in dreams
I have forgotten what she looked like
so that's something. Her eternal twenty
-ness, the eager curl of her smile, her eyes
in which so little could hide
the whole sprawling mural of her
a sketch now: charcoal lines, smudges.
What time has done.
There's a mercy in there somewhere
if only I could find it.

I Have Issues with God

Why the distances left between us
are so vast our souls impossible
to reach worse than stars
and our days too short
to learn much of anything.

Why love dies and regret lives.

Why forgiveness was promised
but we cannot even see how
to forgive ourselves.

Why we walk the world with fear
and uncertainty and not wonder.

Why words fail to carry light
then fail altogether.

Why presence must always be replaced
by absence and absence
becomes presence
and we carry it across our shoulders
like fresh venison
that grows heavier
with each step.

Why revelation has vanished dried up
if it was ever really here
and not just talked into being
by influencers.

Why there are far too many variations
to count that some will disappear
before we get to them
and no one will notice
and their stories not be told.

I could go on but I can see now
how easy it must have been
to lose interest and leave us
to the unforeseen

and move on
no one knows where
another table perhaps
where the luck might be better.

I Have This Life

I am standing in it arms
slipped through its sleeves backwards
like a hospital gown I don't dare go any
-where without it even if I could I can't
explain but sometimes when the neighbors
are sleeping we climb a ladder to the roof
and stand together on hope's edge and
look up count the stars until we're completely
out of numbers frankly I'm not certain
if this life that counts so much is the one
I was meant to have I see everything
through its eyes so it's hard to be objective
things just seem slightly off as if it had
forgotten to tell me something important
and anyway the sky shifts we shift
constellations wheel off in despair and I
forget where we began why it seemed
at first so important to begin why the stars
appeared so near and the air so warm
I have counted off each night like a score
-keeper watching the clock and it's only
now that I see I am running out of time

Stupid Hats

New Year you are a tired old trope
whose nails have grown too long
who can stand you anymore
you stir in your stale sheets and sour smoke
-scent wondering what all the fuss was about
the fuss was about hope pal *Happiness*
our rescue flare our operating-room transfusion
the next thrilling installment a hot futures market
Opening Day
that's why the hoopla
that's why the confetti and the balloons of many colors
the stupid hats

let's face it
you're nothing but an excuse to have a party
and a party has never changed anything
except how we felt in the morning
rarely better
and what do you do from here except stretch out like pastry dough
thinning with each desultory day
I don't know why we ever bothered

henceforth and forever let hope be on us
let us get up early and make our beds without griping
let us put on our yoga pants and pursue the lotus-sweat
    of happiness
and while we're at it let us *carpe diem* a bit too
each day for no one knows the end
why waste one

but when time circles back 'round like a drain
and coos in our ears as it does
let no one blame us if we want to dust off our wits again
and laugh in your feckless face
a small gathering at home this time
to pop the cork on our fizzy anesthetics
so that we can for just a few cozy fireside
-hours forget that every butter-bright tomorrow
always always always
brings death

An Ode to What I Think

I.

I think the World should get a grip.
I think the World whines too much.
I think the World should stop talking *all the time*
and give someone else a chance.

I think People should wise up.
I think they should not read books that make them sad
and self-important in their sadness.
I think they should consider keeping their opinions to themselves
or at least confined to chat rooms.

II.

If Your Mother finds a joint in your shirt pocket
and blames Your Brother for hiding it there, don't argue Logic.
If a Poet lights a candle in a clay bottle and opens the window
for Inspiration to clamber in, do not buy His Book.
If the Moon asks, *is it half-full or half-empty*, don't answer;
it's a trick question, and No One ever gets it right.

III.

I think you, Dear Reader, might be an Abstraction to Others
a cloud, and they see what they want to see in you, or need to.
And I think Faulkner was right, the Past is never past
unless a Flipper buys it and guts it for a profit.

IV.

I think that Children should be seen *and* heard.
I think that Children are sometimes eaten by Bigger Children,
or they grow and are gone, and without them
Spring seems so far away.

I think I should go to a Dodger game
bring my four-year-old in shorts
wait for twilight and the warm breeze out to left
and watch him begin to dream.

Night Moves in from All Sides

Those with nothing left to steal sleep without locks.
Those without ceilings listen all night to the sky, which may fall.
Others with no country curl into themselves
with one eye open and do not dream.

Those who have been broken can never answer
to their satisfaction *why* before shadows bleed
and they see themselves still broken.
Others cannot put down their longing long enough.

Those with regrets sleep only with their regrets.
Those who are too old wake too early.
Some will sleep the sleep of the unsuspecting.
Some will lie down and live a life not their own.

Others will find themselves falling into the world's
restless pent-up embrace, because the world trembles
and burns like a woman who still believes in love.
Somewhere, not here, not now, someone else's dreams

will open before him into infinite aching darkness.

Night Train

In the old brick in windows still lit late
I can see for just a moment faces

staring into darkness and this sudden
light threading through it picking up speed

and wonder if they can see mine staring
back as a mirror stares I want to stop

to step off to stay to climb the stairs to knock
to ask them why they are there in the windows

when others are sleeping ask what it is
they think they might see out here

in the passing darkness that would make things
good enough to rise up in daylight

I want to ask when they are alone like this
with just their heart what does it say

is it anything like mine?

Post-Love Apocalypse

At first I didn't miss it as if my daughter
had only taken a couple of ones
from my wallet and not the fifty
then it became apparent that other things
had begun to disappear with it a great divorce
photographs from the hallway
the better of my two hammers Streisand records
soon my pillow was featherless
emptied of dreams

and God's love off somewhere
in some other universe

at the mall *thy neighbors* wandered
with dull eyes and uncombed hair
and none of them could bring themselves
to buy anything which seemed bad
for the economy and we were all
just going through the motions autonomic
like blinking and breathing in and out only now
there was a nameless ache in our lungs
I couldn't help but wonder what
would take love's place
if anything

if we were all in for a bad time hate
and not hope or exhaustion settling in
or maybe year-round nuclear winter
where no one dared have a night out
would children even bother to be born
or remain formless and breathless
I admit I didn't like our odds

there's a vista point on a steep cliff
up the coast road a few hours' drive
a turnout where lovers and suicides
would go to step into their yearning
and I confess I stopped there and looked down
for a long time listening to the ceaseless
traffic of wave upon wave and to the wind

at waves' end drained of purpose
stumbling up the abrupt yellow edge
of the world searching everywhere
for one last thing

then I saw her standing at the rail
the wind made whole at last in her hair
she too was listening her lips an isthmus
waiting to be crossed

Darkness

I wore a darkness
so dense you could stumble
beneath it and lose your way
which is how it happens
it happens like that
and you wonder whose doing it is
is it yours and what it was
exactly that brought you there
to this place
this decaying dressed-down place
and what can be done now
to get you out of it
wonder whether by luck or force
of will or merely time letting go
will it lift like a curfew at dawn
and what will you have
to show for it but life used up
I tell you this to say it's passed
is firmly in the past
a scorpion trapped in amber
and will stay there
sorrow's flag will snap
on its pole has already snapped
and love's carnival will pack
and leave town has already left
and a hole in the earth will open
like hunger has already opened
and I will not go under
I will walk instead along a stream
lulled by the lullaby it croons
and the surprised laughter
of leaves huddled over
a bird will drop
and sip the still shallows
and there will be light
everywhere
light

www.ingramcontent.com/pod-product-compliance
Lightning Source LLC
LaVergne TN
LVHW090539110826
845146LV00003B/1175